ADVENTURES IN
ANCIENT GREECE

Written by **Linda Bailey**
Illustrated by **Bill Slavin**

Kids Can Press

This book is for my friend and writing colleague, Deborah Hodge,
with thanks for her insight and advice, lo these many books. — L.B.

For Graham, the God of Agility — B.S.

Acknowledgments
We are very grateful to Dr. Mark Golden of the University of Winnipeg
and Dr. M. Eleanor Irwin of the University of Toronto, who reviewed the manuscript
and art for accuracy. Both were generous with their time and advice.
Thanks are also due to the wonderful team at Kids Can Press,
and especially to Valerie Wyatt, for her patience and expertise as an editor,
and Julia Naimska, for her care with the book's design.
A very special thanks goes to the book's first readers: Nico Lauck Stephenson,
Jeremie Lauck Stephenson, Dylan Maxwell and Ian McLellan.
And finally, the author thanks her family (Bill, Lia and Tess) for their ongoing support.

Text © 2002 Linda Bailey
Illustrations © 2002 Bill Slavin

Kids Can Press acknowledges the financial support of the Ontario Arts Council,
the Canada Council for the Arts and the Government of Canada,
through the BPIDP, for our publishing activity.

Published in Canada by   Published in the U.S. by
Kids Can Press Ltd.   Kids Can Press Ltd.
29 Birch Avenue   2250 Military Road
Toronto, ON M4V 1E2   Tonawanda, NY 14150

www.kidscanpress.com

The artwork in this book was rendered in pen and ink and watercolor.
The text is set in Veljovic Book.

Edited by Valerie Wyatt
Designed by Julia Naimska
Printed and bound in China

The hardcover edition of this book is smyth sewn casebound.
The paperback edition of this book is limp sewn with a drawn-on cover.

CM 02 0 9 8 7 6 5 4 3 2 1
CM PA 02 0 9 8 7 6 5 4 3 2

National Library of Canada Cataloguing in Publication Data

Bailey, Linda, 1948–
Adventures in ancient Greece

(Good Times Travel Agency)
ISBN-13: 978-1-55074-534-4 (bound) ISBN-10: 1-55074-534-4 (bound)
ISBN-13: 978-1-55074-536-8 (pbk.) ISBN-10: 1-55074-536-0 (pbk.)

I. Slavin, Bill II. Title. III. Series: Bailey, Linda, 1948–. Good Times Travel Agency.

DF77.B263 2002   j938   C2001-902828-8

Kids Can Press is a **corus** TM Entertainment company

The Binkerton twins — Josh and Emma — stood outside the Good Times Travel Agency with their little sister, Libby. They stared nervously at the door, and who could blame them? Every time they went through that door, they ended up traveling to some long-ago civilization. They ran into danger! They faced disaster! They barely escaped death!

But Josh had an exciting idea. For years he had dreamed of seeing the Olympic Games. Why not time travel to see them — into the future? The Binkertons could be the first kids ever to watch the *next* Olympic Games!

First, though, he had to convince Emma.

Emma couldn't hold out forever. Before she knew it, she was through the door, inside the agency — and under the nose of Julian T. Pettigrew, the owner.

Customers? Come in, come in. No time like the present.

You can say that again.

4

Josh worked up his courage and told Mr. Pettigrew why they'd come.

Eh?

We want to go forward in time, sir — to the next Olympic Games.

Josh did his best to explain ... but it was hard to compete with Libby.

Sports? Every four years? The Olympic Ga—

LIBBY!

Mr. Pettigrew must have gotten the message because he headed for his bookcase of travel guidebooks.

Josh and Emma were so rattled by Libby's behavior, they didn't bother to look closely at the title of the Guidebook. This was a mistake. A *big* mistake!

With a shiver of excitement, Josh flung the book open. There was a terrible, wonderful flash and …

... the Binkertons were there!

But where, exactly, was there?

This didn't look *anything* like the Olympic Games they'd seen on TV! They quickly checked the Guidebook.

This is a battlefield! What are we doing here?

I don't belieeeve it! We're in ancient Greece — where the Olympics first began!

JULIAN T. PETTIGREW'S PERSONAL GUIDE TO ANCIENT GREECE

WELCOME to ancient Greece — an excellent holiday choice.

But what terrible timing! You seem to have arrived right in the middle of a battle.

Unfortunately, battles happen here all the time. Greece in the fifth century B.C. is made up of several hundred city-states (cities plus the countryside around them). These city-states don't always get along. Mostly they fight over farm land, which is scarce in Greece because of all the mountains.

The foot soldiers in a Greek battle are called hoplites. They wear bronze armor, and their fighting style is simple. They pack themselves together, eight rows deep, in a formation called a phalanx. When the bugle sounds, they jog forward together.

Sticking together is important! Each hoplite carries a shield called a hoplon. And as long as they fight shoulder-to-shoulder, hoplites are protected by their neighbors' shields as well as their own.

Eventually, the two sides come together with a mighty crash! The front soldiers start jabbing the enemy with their spears. The back soldiers try to push the front soldiers forward, through the enemy line. War cries fill the air! Swords come out! It's brutal, it's ferocious, and the very worst spot is in the middle!

If you're watching a battle, be careful — and whatever you do, don't *ever* get stuck between two lines of hoplites.

But there was no time to talk. The battle lines were getting closer. The Binkertons were about to become the filling in a soldier sandwich! Frantically, they searched for cover.

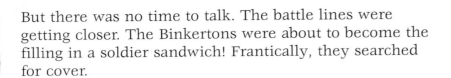

I hate it when this happens.

This is going to hurt. This is really going to hurt.

The Binkertons waited to be crushed like walnuts between the two opposing armies. But minutes passed ... and nothing happened.

I think they're leaving.

CITY-STATES — SEPARATE, BUT STILL GREEK

Greece is a land of steep mountains and lonely islands, so the city-states are mostly cut off from each other. No wonder they don't get along!

Each city-state is like a tiny separate country. It has the same language, religion, beliefs and general customs as its neighbors, but it's not united with them in any way. Most people are fiercely loyal to their own city-state. They're ready to defend it — to the death if necessary.

Athens and Sparta are the two main city-states.

A man wearing a wreath on his head seemed to be the center of attention. Creeping closer, the Binkertons discovered that he was announcing a truce.

I love this guy!

You must cease your fighting until the Olympic Games are over.

All Emma felt was relief. The truce would give them enough time to read the Guidebook so they could go home.

But Josh was still eager to see some Olympic Games. He didn't even mind if they were ancient!

It's a once-in-a-lifetime opportunity.

I just want to have a lifetime.

Still, the people who live in city-states *are* all Greeks. From time to time, they get together at all-Greek festivals where they honor their gods by competing in sporting contests. One of these festivals is the Olympic Games, which take place every four years.

When it's time for the Olympic Games, the Greek city-states put aside their quarrels. Truce-bearers travel all over the Greek world to tell people the date of the festival and to announce that wars must stop. Anyone who wants to travel to the Games can do so without fear. This time of peace is called the Olympic truce.

Following a group of soldiers, the Binkertons eventually arrived at the edge of a city. They stopped the first friendly looking person they saw.

Is this the Olympic Games?

Oh no. They're held at Olympia. This is Athens — the most glorious city in the world.

ATHENS

Looking for action? Be sure to visit Athens. In the fifth century B.C., it's definitely the place to be. With more than 250 000 people, it's the largest Greek city-state. It's also the richest and most powerful.

Like other Greek cities, Athens is circled by high walls. (After seeing that last battle, you'll understand why.) It's on the Aegean Sea and has an excellent port. Ships come and go all the time. Busy, busy, busy.

Plan to spend at least a day or two looking around. Athens is a magnificent center of art and culture, admired all through Greece and beyond. People come here to learn from the best artists, the best architects, the best dramatists, the best teachers, the best —

But don't listen to me. See for yourself.

(It's downright glorious!)

12

The boy, whose name was Demeas, promised to help the Binkertons get to the Olympics. First, though, he insisted on showing them around Athens — starting with a hill called the Pnyx.

Emma listened politely. But Josh had a one-track mind — and guess who was on the track?

It doesn't look like much now, but when there's an assembly, thousands of men come here to vote.

Men? Just men?

YAY, JOSH!

BRAVO! AMAZING!

DEMOCRACY IN ATHENS

Are you at the Pnyx yet? Pay close attention. History is being made here!

Greece is the first place where ordinary people get to rule their own country. The ancient Greeks call this kind of government "demokratia" ("demos" means people, and "kratos" means power). Later in history, it will be called "democracy."

Here's how it works. There's no king here. No president or prime minister either. Instead, ordinary citizens have a huge meeting every nine or ten days on the Pnyx and vote on things. It's called the Assembly. Anyone can speak. The audience laughs, hisses, boos or claps for the speakers. Then they vote by raising their hands.

But wait a minute! Not *everyone* gets to vote. You have to be male, free (not a slave) and born to Athenian parents. This means no women can vote. Neither can the thousands of slaves, or people who have come here from other places.

Well, okay, democracy here isn't perfect. But it *is* an important contribution of the ancient Greeks. Democracy will grow and spread all over the world.

13

Demeas loved his city and was a very enthusiastic tour guide. This would have been terrific — if the Binkertons had *wanted* a tour guide.

The next thing they knew, they were at a theater where a play was being rehearsed.

Isn't it magnificent?

Sure. Great. Magnificent. Can we go to the Olympics now?

Libby? Where's —? *LIBBY!* You get OUT of there.

GREEK THEATER

Here's another "first" for the ancient Greeks — the world's first theaters! Don't expect a movie, though. Greek theaters show live performances of plays. They're built outdoors on hillsides and have seats for up to 14 000 people, packed in like sardines.

Try to get a seat near the front. But if you end up in the back row, don't worry. Greek theaters are built so that sound will carry, even without microphones (which won't be invented for another few thousand years).

Greek plays may look a little strange to you. For one thing, there are usually no more than three main actors. Each actor may play several roles, wearing different masks. There's also a group of guys called the chorus who sing, dance and speak to the audience.

Guys? Did I say "guys"? Greek theater has only male actors — even for the female roles. (Sorry, girls.)

Josh was more than ready to leave Athens, but Demeas wouldn't hear of it! Promising his new friends a delicious treat, he hurried them along to the marketplace.

Olives! The best in the world.

This is a treat?

I think I'll ... er ... save mine for later.

THE AGORA

Would you like to buy some flowers? Fish? Fruit? Firewood? Footwear? Come to the marketplace! It's called the agora, and you can buy (or sell) almost anything here.

But the agora isn't just a market. It's also a meeting place and the heart of any Greek city. People get together with friends here and chat about business or government — or just share the latest gossip. Pick a shady spot under one of the stoas (long open buildings with columns) and start talking. The Athenians are great talkers.

If you have extra cash, bring it along. There are bankers and moneylenders who would love to meet you and your Athenian money (silver coins with owls stamped on them). Don't have a wallet? Try carrying your money ancient Greek style — in your mouth.

Blechh!

The marketplace was a great place to meet people, and the Binkertons soon met some Greek philosophers.

They were very interesting. (Well, not really.)

What is justice?

What should human beings aim for?

What do we mean when we say that something exists?

What do I have to do to get to the Olympics?

GREEK PHILOSOPHERS

Thinking of leaving Athens? Think again. Think hard!

You won't be the only one thinking in ancient Greece. People here love to think — and to discuss what they're thinking about. The ancient Greeks are a curious bunch, eager to know about the world and how it works. Some think about the stars and nature. Others think about mathematical problems. Still others think about people and how they should behave. Some try to answer difficult questions such as "What is beauty?" and "What is love?"

These ancient Greek thinkers are called philosophers ("lovers of wisdom"). They like to travel around, teaching their ideas to others. Watch for them in the agora, sitting around in small groups, arguing and discussing ... and thinking, of course. If you're in a thoughtful mood, join in. Or maybe you'd rather just listen and ...

Hey! YOU! Wake up! PAY ATTENTION!

The ideas of the most famous Greek philosophers (Socrates, Plato, Aristotle) are important. They will last for a very long time, so LISTEN UP!

Emma noticed that she wasn't seeing many women in Athens.

They're at home, of course.

What does he mean — of course?

CLAP! CLAP!

When she spotted some girls at a fountain, she stopped to say hello.

Why aren't you at home?

We are slaves. We have work to do.

Seeing how heavy their jars were, Emma offered to help.

No, wait! I can do it!

But there are times when being helpful just isn't very ... helpful.

You wouldn't happen to have a tube of Wonder Glue? Er, no, I guess not.

GREEK SOCIETY

Who's who in ancient Athens?

Basically, there are two groups: male citizens who get to vote and ... everyone else (women, slaves and foreigners)!

Women generally marry young (at 14 or 15), and spend their lives at home, running their households. The only time most Athenian women get out is for funerals and religious festivals (fortunately, there are plenty), or to visit relatives and close friends.

Athenian families generally have at least one or two slaves who do most of the household work. Well-educated slaves might tutor the family's children. Slaves also work in the family business or on the family farm. Some slaves come from outside Greece, captured by slave traders. Others are the children of slaves.

Finally, there are the metics — people who come to live in Athens from elsewhere. Some run businesses and are quite rich. Metics can never be citizens. Like women and slaves, they will never be able to vote.

(Neither can you, no matter how long you stay here. Forget it.)

17

Emma did her best to enjoy herself in Athens …

And most glorious of all is — the Parthenon!

Oh, my! It really is glorious.

Very nice. Now what about those Games?

… but she was definitely having a bad day. Maybe even a bad century! When some Greek garbage got tossed, she was right in its path.

Not … having … fun.

Marvelous!

Can I drive?

THE PARTHENON

Look up. Look way up. That rocky hill overlooking the city is called the Acropolis. To the Athenians, it's a sacred area. That large building on top, made of creamy white marble, is called the Parthenon. It was built to honor Athena, goddess of Athens.

Take a close look at the Parthenon's columns. They look straight, right? Guess what? They're not. Straight columns would look saggy from a distance. In order to make the Parthenon's columns *look* straight, the builders made them bulge in the middle. It's an optical illusion!

Inside the Parthenon is a huge statue of Athena covered with ivory and gold. Outside is an even larger bronze Athena, holding a gold-tipped spear. She's like a beacon to sailors, who can see her from far out at sea.

Things went from bad to worse when Demeas invited the Binkertons home. They were barely through the door when Emma and Libby got whisked away.

Please join us in the women's quarters.

Women's what? Wait a — JOSH!

AN ANCIENT GREEK HOME

Tired? Why not relax in the home of a local family? Don't expect anything fancy, though. Houses here are made of mud bricks covered with plaster. Floors are stone or dirt.

Houses of wealthier Greeks have two floors. Downstairs is the andron (men's dining room) where the men of the house entertain friends. Upstairs is the gynaeconitis (women's area) where women, children and female slaves work and play.

In the center is an open courtyard. Look for an altar to the main Greek god, Zeus. There might also be a well for water.

Furniture is simple — mainly stools, benches and chests. There are also wooden couches covered in cushions and blankets, with small tables that fit underneath. Clay lamps, filled with olive oil, keep things bright in the evening.

Why would things need to be bright? Well, you just never know. There *might* be a party!

That evening, there was a dinner party at Demeas's house, with plenty of food, drink and entertainment. Emma enjoyed the music … from a distance.

But Josh got a close-up look.

The party went on and on ... with talking and eating ... and talking and poetry ... and talking and drinking ... and talking and music ... and more talking. It was the longest party that Emma had ever not been invited to.

I wish I could go to the party.

I wish I could go to sleep!

FOOD & DINNER PARTIES

Hungry? Lie down and have something to eat! Ancient Greek food is simple and healthy — bread or porridge (made from barley or wheat), fruit, vegetables and cheese. Most Greeks also enjoy seafood, eggs and poultry — and all the olives they can eat.

Meat is eaten mostly on special occasions such as festivals and weddings. Try an olive, instead. Don't like olives? Oh, dear. Greece is serious olive-growing country. You'd better *start* liking them.

The ancient Greeks often have dinner parties called symposia. (Sorry, they're only for men.)

Guests at a symposium take off their sandals and lie on couches to eat. They wear garlands on their heads and are waited on by slaves.

What do you do at a symposium? You eat, of course. (There'll be plenty of olives.) For drinks, there's wine mixed with water. Sometimes there are entertainers. Other times, guests provide their own entertainment — singing, reciting poetry, asking riddles or playing games. Here's a game for you! Wait till your cup is almost empty and then flick what's left at a target. It's called kottabos.

First thing next morning, the Binkertons cornered Demeas and demanded his help to get to Olympia. It turned out he was traveling there himself, on his uncle's boat.

He invited Josh along — but not the girls.

That did it! Now Emma was determined to go to the Olympic Games, even if she had to walk every step of the way.

Olympia turned out to be a long, long, *long* walk away. The road was rough and hilly.

Hasn't anyone here ever heard of a bus?

There had to be an easier way. Josh thought he'd found it when he met a group of travelers from Sparta.

They have horses — and carts! Come on!

Carts? Can I drive?

GETTING AROUND IN ANCIENT GREECE

Need to travel in ancient Greece? Here's a word of advice. Water! Traveling by water is by far the easiest way to go. On a ship, you can quickly "hop" from island to island across the sea. With a good wind, you can travel 240 kilometers (150 miles) a day.

If you have to go by land, too bad. There are few roads in this mountainous country, and those that exist are steep, rocky and full of ruts. When the Olympic Games are on, the roads are crowded, too. Try to get a hold of a mule or a donkey to carry your belongings. Maybe a passing ox-cart will give you a lift.

Chances are, though, you'll have to walk. (Have an olive. It will cheer you up.)

23

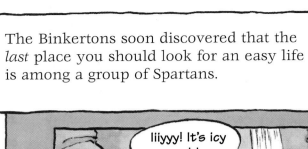

The Binkertons soon discovered that the *last* place you should look for an easy life is among a group of Spartans.

Iiiyyy! It's icy cold.

Icy is good!

The icier, the better!

There's a nice soft grassy spot right over there.

He doesn't want a nice soft grassy spot, Josh.

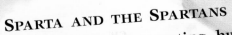

SPARTA AND THE SPARTANS

The Athenians are interesting, but if you really want an adventure, get to know some Spartans!

Sparta is a powerful Greek city-state and quite different from the others. For one thing, all Spartan men are professional soldiers. They spend all their time fighting and training for war. (The citizens of other city-states work as farmers or craftsmen and only fight part-time.)

It's not easy being raised a Spartan. When you're born, the elders check you over. If you look weak or sick, you may be left on a nearby mountain to die. If you're a boy, you'll be taken from your mother at about age seven to live in army barracks and train as a soldier.

You'll be expected to put up with cold, pain and hunger and become a tough Spartan warrior. You'll go barefoot and have to eat black broth — a horrible soup made of pork, pig's blood and vinegar. It's famous all over Greece for its nastiness.

Don't expect your mother to help you. Spartan women are raised to be strong and to produce tough warrior sons. Your mother will send you off to war, telling you to come home *with* your shield (a brave soldier) or *on* your shield (a dead soldier!). If you're cowardly and lose your shield, don't come home at all. There are stories of Spartan mothers killing their sons for cowardice.

Leaving the Spartans behind, the Binkertons straggled on alone. But as they got close to Olympia, Josh began to worry. What if Emma and Libby weren't allowed to watch the Games?

It wasn't hard to make Libby look like a boy ...

26

ANCIENT GREEK CLOTHING & HAIRSTYLES

Man, woman or child — in ancient Greece, you'll wear a chiton. It's a simple rectangle of wool or linen cloth fastened at the shoulders and sides, leaving gaps for your head and arms. A soft belt around your waist finishes it off. Women wear their chitons ankle-length, but slaves, children and working men wear them shorter, to the knees. In cool weather, you can also wear a himation (cloak) over your chiton. Add a pair of sandals, and — presto! — you're a well-dressed ancient Greek.

Hairstyles are more complicated. Men generally have short hair and beards, while boys grow their hair long — except in Sparta, where boys have short hair and men have long hair. Women and girls wear their hair very long. Before marriage, they wear it in ringlets. After marriage, they pile it up on top of their heads with ribbons, pins and decorations.

See what I mean? Hair is complicated. But don't worry about it. Just try to stay cool. Summers in Greece can get very, very hot. Aren't you glad your clothes are loose and light?

27

And so, Emma entered the ancient Olympic Games "undercover." She and Josh got some strange looks ... but nobody stopped them.

OLYMPIA

Welcome, welcome, welcome to the greatest spectacle in ancient Greece! Join the thousands who come to Olympia to watch the Olympic Games. They're held once every four years to honor the god Zeus. (There are other games to honor different gods, but the Olympics are the greatest.)

Take a look around. Olympia isn't a city. It's a grassy plain in the countryside, dotted with trees and shrubs. Start by touring the Altis, a sacred area filled with temples, altars and statues. Be sure to see:

1. The Great Temple of Zeus (containing a magnificent statue of Zeus, one of the Seven Wonders of the Ancient World).

The Binkertons did their best to blend in.

Such long legs! Will you be running in the Games?

Er ... only if I have to.

Air ... give me air ...

Hey, guys! Good to see you. Great games, eh?

Getting really hot in here.

2. The sacred olive tree, from which winners' wreaths are cut by a boy with a golden sickle.
3. The Temple of Hera, Zeus's wife.
4. The Great Altar of Zeus.

Nearby are the Stadium (running track for foot races) and the Hippodrome (horse track). Get to these tracks early to see the races! And now for the bad news. Do not expect to be comfortable while you're here. It's midsummer and scorching hot. There are flies everywhere. It's crowded, dusty and noisy. There's nowhere to wash and hardly anywhere to sleep (except outside). The drinking water is likely stagnant, and you'll probably *never* find a toilet.

Aside from all that ... it's a very nice place. Enjoy!

When the Binkertons sat down to watch the Games, they got a big surprise.

THE OLYMPIC GAMES

Don't just stand there, gaping. Find a place to sit. Forty thousand people are competing with you for the best viewing spot, so hurry!

Settled? Good. If you're wearing a hat, take it off. Hats block people's views and are forbidden here.

As you watch these ancient Games, you'll probably notice some differences from the modern Olympics. For instance:
- No team sports.
- No water sports.
- No clothes!

No clothes for the athletes, anyway. In the ancient Olympic Games, they compete naked. One explanation is that long ago an athlete's clothing fell off during a race. When he won, he started a new fashion.

But clothing or not, the Games were definitely exciting! In fact, they were so exciting that the Binkertons soon forgot the athletes' (missing) uniforms.

Following the crowds from event to event, they watched as much as they could.

WRESTLING

RUNNING

BOXING

32

PENTATHLON

PANKRATION

Do your best to see the main events while you are here. Aside from the equestrian (horse) sports, they are:

- Running — a short sprint, a longer sprint and a long race
- Wrestling — a contest requiring skill and grace
- Boxing — a match between boxers wearing leather strips around their hands
- Pentathlon — a five-sport event that includes running, long jump, wrestling, javelin-throwing and discus-throwing
- Pankration — a vicious combination of wrestling and boxing

If you don't like violence, stay away from the pankration. Competitors are allowed to punch, hit, wrestle, twist arms, break fingers, even strangle their opponents. Some pankratiasts actually lose their lives!

There are also separate events for boys 12 to 18 and a race in armor for hoplite soldiers who clank and clatter down the track.

And the grand prize for the winner of any Olympic event is ... a wreath of olive branches! (Doesn't sound like much? Don't worry. Winners are very well treated by their city-states when they go home.)

33

In the end, Josh and Emma got so interested in the Games that they stopped paying attention to their little sister.

This was a big mistake.

It's the chariot races!

Libby? Where's Libby?

EQUESTRIAN EVENTS

Ready for a wild ride? Hurry down to the Hippodrome (horse track) to see the equestrian (horse) events.

The horse races are a big thrill here at the ancient Olympics. Saddles and stirrups haven't yet been invented, so the jockeys ride bareback with their feet hanging loose. Is it hard to hang on? Is it hard to control the horse? You bet!

The chariot races are even more exciting — and dangerous. There are two kinds of races — two-horse and four-horse. It's a rough, tooth-jarring ride. The Hippodrome isn't circular like a modern racetrack. It's a straight track, so the chariots have to go back and forth, turning around a post at each end.

That's where it gets really dangerous — at the posts. If, by some chance, you end up driving a chariot (a very bad idea, by the way), TRY TO STAY AHEAD ON THE TURNS! Terrible things can happen if you don't. Your wheels could lock! Your chariot might flip! You could smash into other chariots — or the post! Even if you don't crash, it will be *crazy* out there, with shouting drivers, straining horses, clouds of dust and nasty pileups.

No wonder this is the most dangerous event in the whole ancient Olympics! (It's also one of the most popular.)

Libby managed to hang on for two laps. She even took the lead! But, like many charioteers, she had a little trouble on the turns.

Josh and Emma ran as quickly as possible — not very quickly, of course — to the middle of the Hippodrome. By the time they got there, Libby was gone.

Have you seen a little gir ... er, boy ... about this big?

Josh and Emma would have been desperate with worry if they hadn't known their sister so well.

She's hiding somewhere. I'm sure of it!

There!

Libby was now the least popular person in all of Olympia. Josh and Emma realized that they would have to sneak her out. There was only one way.

Are you sure this will work?

No problem!

Big problem!

Trying to find their way out of Olympia, the Binkertons got caught up in a huge crowd. It carried them toward a tall altar — and what looked like the biggest barbecue Josh had ever seen!

Holy smoke!

Exactly!

With Libby hidden under his chiton, Josh was not only tall; he was also lumpy.

Shouldn't have eaten all those olives.

GREEK RELIGION & SACRIFICES

With so many sports going on, it's easy to forget that the Olympic Games are first of all a religious festival. They're held to honor the god Zeus, whom the Greeks believe to be ruler of the world.

The ancient Greeks have many gods. The twelve most important are believed to live on Mount Olympus, the highest mountain in Greece. They include Zeus (god of the sky and weather), Poseidon (ruler of the seas), Hera (goddess of women and marriage), and Aphrodite (goddess of love). The ancient Greeks believe that these gods have power over

their lives and can help or harm them. To keep the gods happy, people offer prayers and sacrifices. They also hold festivals (such as the Olympic Games).

During the Olympic Games, there is a great sacrifice to Zeus. A hundred oxen are slaughtered, and their thigh bones are burned on an altar as a gift to Zeus, who is thought to enjoy the smoke. The rest of the oxen meat is roasted and eaten by spectators. Stick around and look hungry — there may be a spare rib for you. (Believe me, Zeus will never miss it.)

The Binkertons hadn't had much to eat during the Games, so they hung around. When the barbecued meat was handed out, Josh quickly made up for lost time.

His sisters weren't so lucky.

It took a few pinches from his sisters, but Josh did find a way to share.

The Greeks were definitely getting suspicious. Still, it might have been all right except for ...

Libby!

The Binkertons' secret was out —

— and the chase was on!

There were many fine runners at the ancient Olympics. Some may have run *faster* than the Binkertons. But none ever ran harder.

They ran to the only hiding place they knew.

The Binkertons had a problem. They were ready to go home, but they had to stay hidden — and as long as they were hidden, they couldn't finish the Guidebook and go home!

The Binkertons waited and waited for a chance to leave. But before they could make a move ... their hiding places began to move.

For a long time, the Binkertons rolled around inside their containers. Then, suddenly, the jars began to move in a whole different way.

They were on a ship! It was noisy and crowded, and it was moving very quickly.

Why is it so crowded?

I think it's a warship.

WHAT??

GREEK WARSHIPS

Why not end your visit to ancient Greece with a relaxing cruise on a trireme? A trireme is a warship, but don't be nervous. The Olympic truce is still on, so you'll be perfectly safe. Come aboard!

A trireme is long, light and narrow. It has space (barely) for 170 rowers, jammed in below deck like sardines. They sit in three levels to keep from hitting one another's oars.

A trireme is more than a ship. It's also a weapon. With its jutting point and sharp blades at the front, it's designed for ramming. It can crash head-on into the side of an enemy ship. It can also be rowed alongside, close enough to slice off the enemy's oars.

Triremes have a huge eye painted on each side to protect the ship against evil, so they're easy to spot. If you see other triremes on your cruise, give them a wave. As long as the Olympic truce is in effect, you're perfectly safe.

Unless, of course, someone *breaks* the truce ...

44

The Binkertons read as they had never read before. They read so fast, sparks flew off the pages. But the other ship was racing toward them! It was — COMING — THROUGH — THE — SIDE!!! The Binkertons ...

The Binkertons vowed right then and there that the only Olympic Games they would watch in future would be on TV.

As they walked out the door of the Good Times Travel Agency, they made a second vow.

But *never*? Well, that's a very long time.

Even for time travelers.

ANCIENT GREECE

Fact or fantasy?

How much can you believe of *Adventures in Ancient Greece?*

The Binkerton kids are made up. Their adventures are made up, too. So the story of the Binkertons is just that — a story.

But there really were ancient Greeks, who invented theater and held the first Olympic Games and ... well, if you really want to know, read the Guidebook! That's where you'll find the facts. All the information in Julian T. Pettigrew's Personal Guide to Ancient Greece is based on historical fact.

More about ancient Greece

The ancient Greeks produced one of the most extraordinary civilizations the world has ever seen. It grew up in the same area as two earlier civilizations — the Minoan and the Mycenaean.

You can see the Greek homeland in purple on the map. Around the eighth century B.C., the ancient Greeks formed colonies around the Mediterranean Sea, shown in brown. Trading with other areas made the Greeks prosperous, and they picked up new ideas from neighboring countries.

This set the stage for the height of Greek civilization. It happened about 2500 years ago, in the fifth century B.C, and is sometimes called the Classical Period. It was during this period that the Binkertons visited — a "golden age" of extraordinary new ideas about human beings and the universe. The ancient Greeks produced some of the world's first historians and scientists and made important

contributions to mathematics, astronomy and geography. They started the world's first democracy. Greek philosophers such as Plato and Aristotle had ideas that are still studied today, and a Greek doctor, Hippocrates, is considered the father of western medicine.

In the fourth century B.C, Greece fell under the rule of nearby Macedon. One of its leaders, Alexander the Great, so admired the Greeks that he spread their ideas throughout his vast empire. Later, when the Romans ruled Greece, they also admired Greek culture, copying and developing its art and ideas. Today, ancient Greek culture is seen as the birthplace of western civilization.

We know quite a lot about the ancient Greeks and their Olympic Games ... but not as much as we'd like to. Historians don't have complete information, for example, about the Olympic Truce. Although heralds proclaimed it throughout the Greek world, it's not clear whether the truce protected all city-states from attack, or only Elis (where Olympia was located). Also, the order of Olympic events changed through the years, so we are not positive about that, either. Historians also don't agree on whether a girl like Emma would have been allowed to watch the Games. (Married women were definitely not allowed.)

Do we know everything about the ancient Greeks? No. Will we learn more in future? Probably. Historians and archeologists never stop searching for new information about the past. They would love to travel to ancient Greece. If only they could find the right travel agency ...

In this book:

LITTLE HOUSE

Laura Ingalls Wilder

MY FIRST LITTLE HOUSE BOOKS

DANCE AT GRANDPA'S

ADAPTED FROM THE LITTLE HOUSE BOOKS

By Laura Ingalls Wilder

Illustrated by Renée Graef

HARPERCOLLINS PUBLISHERS

For Rhonda
—R.G.

Dance at Grandpa's   Text adapted from Little House in the Big Woods, *copyright 1932, 1960 Little House Heritage Trust*
Illustrations copyright © 1994 by Renée Graef   Manufactured in China. All rights reserved.
For information address HarperCollins Children's Books, a division of HarperCollins Publishers.
195 Broadway, New York, NY 10007.
Library of Congress Cataloging-in-Publication Data   Wilder, Laura Ingalls, 1867–1957.   Dance at Grandpa's / adapted from the
Little house books by Laura Ingalls Wilder ; illustrated by Renée Graef.   p.   cm. — (My First Little House books)
Summary: A young pioneer girl and her family attend a wintertime party at her grandparents' house in the Big Woods of Wisconsin.
ISBN 0-06-443372-2 (pbk.)   [1. Frontier and pioneer life—Wisconsin—Fiction.   2. Family life—Wisconsin—Fiction.
3. Parties—Fiction.   4. Wisconsin—Fiction.]   I. Graef, Renée, ill.   II. Title.   III. Series: Wilder, Laura Ingalls, 1867–1957.
My first Little House books.   PZ7.W6461Dan 1994   [E]—dc20 · 93-24535   CIP   AC   Typography by Christine Kettner   ❖
HarperCollins®, ▰®, and Little House® are trademarks of HarperCollins Publishers Inc.
15 16 SCP 20

Once upon a time, a little girl named Laura lived in the Big Woods of Wisconsin in a little house made of logs. She lived there with her Pa, her Ma, her big sister Mary, her baby sister Carrie, and their good old bulldog Jack.

One winter morning everyone got up early, for there was going to be a big party at Grandpa's house. While Laura and Mary ate their breakfast, Pa packed his fiddle carefully in its box and put it in the big sled waiting by the gate.

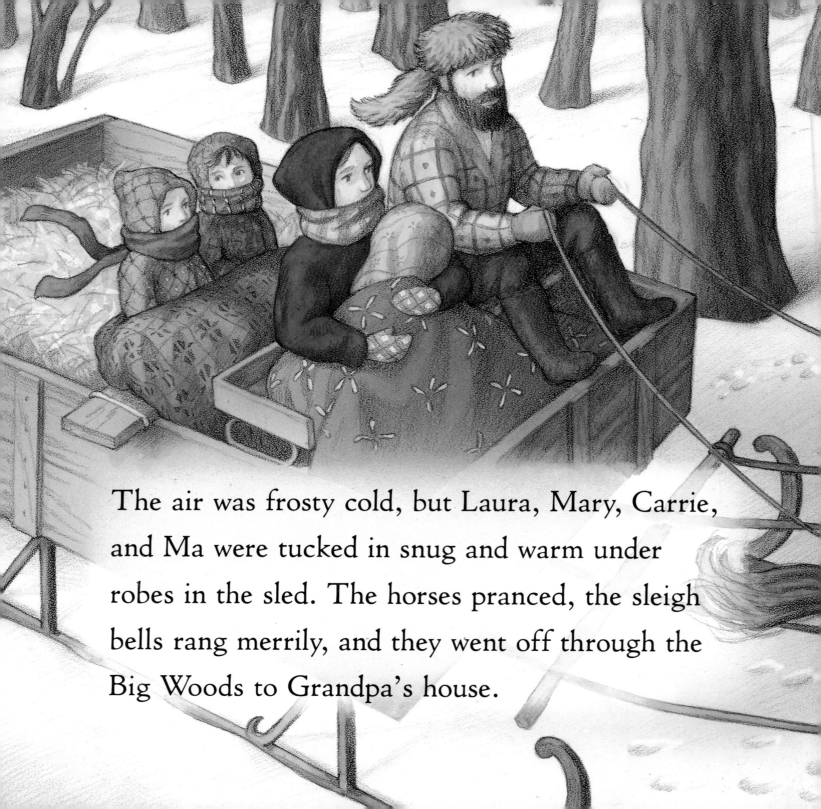

The air was frosty cold, but Laura, Mary, Carrie, and Ma were tucked in snug and warm under robes in the sled. The horses pranced, the sleigh bells rang merrily, and they went off through the Big Woods to Grandpa's house.

It did not seem long before they were sweeping into the clearing at Grandpa's house. Grandma stood at the door smiling and calling them to come in.

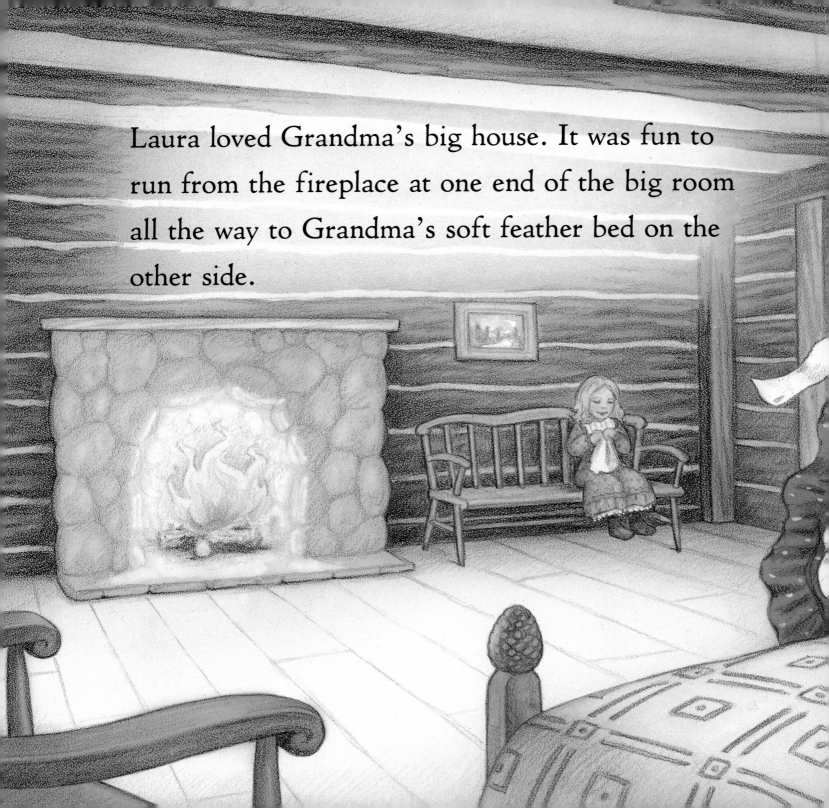

Laura loved Grandma's big house. It was fun to run from the fireplace at one end of the big room all the way to Grandma's soft feather bed on the other side.

The whole house smelled good. There were sweet and spicy smells coming from the kitchen, and the smell of hickory logs burning with bright, clear flames in the fireplace.

Before long it was time to get ready for the party. Laura watched while Ma and the aunts made themselves pretty. They combed their long hair and put on their best dresses. Laura thought Ma was the most beautiful of all in her green ruffled dress.

Soon people began to come to the party. They came on foot through the woods with their lanterns, and they came in sleds and wagons. Sleigh bells were jingling all the time.

The big room was filled with tall boots and
swishing skirts, and there were ever so many babies
lying in rows on Grandma's feather bed. Laura
thought Baby Carrie was the prettiest.

Then Pa took out his fiddle and began to play. All the skirts began to swirl and all the boots began to stamp. "Swing your partners!" Pa called.

Laura watched Ma's skirt swaying and her dark head bowing and thought she was the loveliest dancer in the world.

Soon it was time for dinner. The long table was loaded with pumpkin pies, dried-berry pies, and cookies. There was cold boiled pork and salt-rising bread. How sour the pickles were! They all ate until they could eat no more.

The fiddling and dancing went on and on until it was time for Laura and the other children to go to bed.

When Laura woke up, it was morning. There were pancakes and maple syrup for breakfast, and then Pa brought the horses and sled to the door.

Pa tucked Laura and Mary and Carrie and Ma into the sled. Grandma and Grandpa stood calling, "Good-by! Good-by!" as they rode away into the Big Woods, going home. What a wonderful party it had been!